WEATHER SIGNS

WEATHER REPORT

Ann and Jim Merk

The Rourke Corporation, Inc.
Vero Beach, Florida 32964

PHOTO CREDITS
All photos © Lynn M. Stone

Library of Congress Cataloging-in-Publication Data

Merk, Ann, 1952–
    Weather signs / by Ann and Jim Merk
        p. cm. — (Weather report)
    Includes index
    ISBN 0-86593-388-X
    1. Weather—Folklore—Juvenile literature. [1. Weather—Folklore.]
I. Merk, Jim, 1952- . II. Title   III. Series: Merk, Ann, 1952-   Weather report.
QC998.M47 1994
551.6'31—dc20   94-13323
                                                   CIP
Printed in the USA   AC

TABLE OF CONTENTS

WEATHER SIGNS

What will the **weather** be like tomorrow? Next week? Next month? No one can tell for sure, but people use "signs" of the weather to help make guesses.

Some weather signs are no more than silly, old tales. They don't really tell us anything about the weather to be. Other signs, however, can be quite helpful and provide real clues about weather.

Even on a sunny day, drapes of moss reveal the true climate of the rain forest—wet!

GROUNDHOG DAY

The groundhog, or woodchuck, just may be America's best known weather sign.

Woodchucks spend the cold months in a deep sleep. But according to a legend, the woodchuck pops out of its burrow on February 2, Groundhog Day.

If the woodchuck sees its shadow, it is frightened. It rushes back into its den, and winter continues for six more weeks.

If the woodchuck doesn't see its shadow, it stays out. Legend says that means spring is near.

A groundhog that sees its shadow on February 2 means six more weeks of winter, according to legend

CLOUD SIGNS

Clouds are a much more accurate sign of weather than woodchucks. Puffy white clouds are a sign of fair weather. If the white clouds begin to stack up, thunderstorms are near.

The arrival of high, thin **cirrus** clouds is often a sign that rain clouds will follow.

A pile of puffy clouds growing into thunderheads means a storm is near

RAINBOWS AND WARNINGS

"Rainbow at morning, sailors take warning," goes an old tale. "Rainbow at night, sailors delight."

Unlike the groundhog tale, this one has some truth to it. A rainbow is born when sunlight passes through raindrops. If a sailor saw a rainbow late in the day, the storm would probably pass before morning. A morning rainbow, however, would mean a new storm was brewing.

Waves of geese signal changing seasons

The arrival of skunk cabbage is a sure sign of spring

PLANT SIGNS

Looking at plants can be a preview of a place's long range weather, or **climate**. Certain plants live only in certain weather conditions.

Most wild cactus plants, for example, live only in places where the climate is warm and dry. Orange trees need warm weather, but they also need a cool period. Moss grows only in wet climates.

The bloom of each kind of flower is tied to climate and sunlight. When the skunk cabbage blooms, you know spring is just ahead even if the woodchuck *saw* its shadow!

Orange trees will grow only in certain climates that have no killing frosts

SIGNS ON THE MOUNTAINS

The climate of a tall mountain changes greatly from bottom to top. The plants reveal the changes.

The base of the mountain may have dense forest on one side and desert-like plants on the other. The forest side has a wet climate while the desert side is dry.

Close to the top of the mountain's forest side, the trees are short and bent. Long periods of cold wind have bent the trees and "trimmed" their branches.

The harsh, windy climate on high mountains bends branches and keeps trees short

SIGNS OF THE SEASONS

Each season has its own climate. By watching plants and animals carefully, anyone can tell when the next season is about to begin.

Geese and other birds head south each autumn. Their flight signals summer's farewell.

Winter is just ahead when the coats of certain hares and weasels turn white.

Each spring red-winged blackbirds and northbound swans begin arriving on marshes. Days may be cold, but the birds' activity is a sign that spring is near.

The snowshoe hare's coat begins to whiten long before the snow flies

CLEAR WEATHER AHEAD!

An old weather verse reads, "When dew is on the grass, rain will never pass."

Sooner or later, rain will fall. But dew is often a sign of fair skies, at least for a while.

Dewdrops won't form unless night skies are clear and windless. Without clouds and wind, rain has to wait for another day.

Beads of dew cling to the silk of a spider web on a clear September morning

FISHES AND FLIES

"Before a rain the fishes rise, and nimbly catch uncautious flies." Does the behavior of flies really tell us anything about the weather? Perhaps.

Air heavy with moisture usually means rain. Heavy air forces insects to fly lower because extra moisture settles on their wings. Flying for a bug becomes more of a chore.

Insects that fly close to the water are easy **prey**, or food, for fish.

Glossary

cirrus (SEER us) — thin and wispy white clouds made up of tiny ice particles at high altitudes

climate (KLI mit) — the type of weather conditions that any place has over a long period of time

prey (PRAY) — an animal that is hunted by another animal for food

weather (WEH ther) — what it is like outside on any day at any time

INDEX